Our Active Earth

Written by Matilda May

Flying Start
to Literacy®

T0363511

Contents

Introduction

Look down at the ground under your feet. What are you standing on?

The Earth beneath our feet feels safe and stable. But, in fact, the surface of the Earth is always changing. It slides, cracks and explodes.

This movement and motion can change the environment and wreak havoc on people's lives.

Red-hot lava flows out of the ground when a volcano erupts.

Chapter 1

The rocky Earth

Our planet Earth is a rocky planet. It is made up of rock, but it is not solid rock all the way to the centre. We stand on the solid outer layer called the crust.

Underneath the crust is a layer called the mantle, which is made up of solid rock and hot liquid rock called magma.

Beneath the mantle, at the centre of the Earth, is the core. The core is solid metal surrounded by a layer of hot liquid metal.

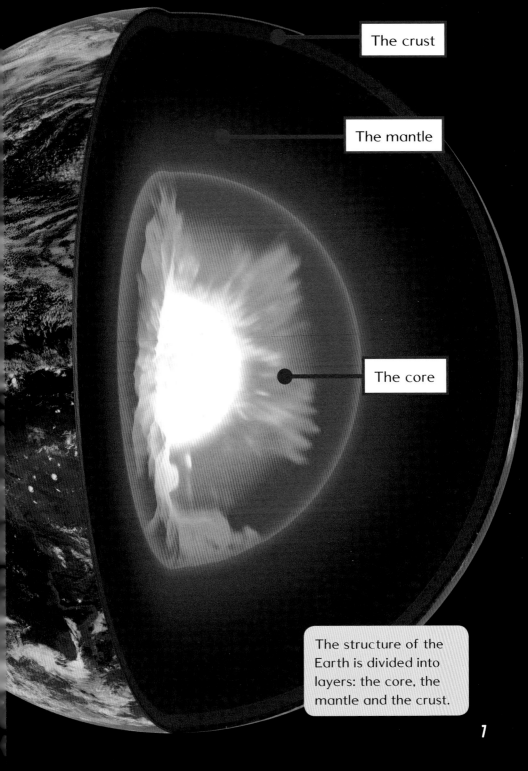

The crust

The mantle

The core

The structure of the Earth is divided into layers: the core, the mantle and the crust.

Tectonic plates and fault lines

People who study changes in the Earth's crust are called geologists. To explain the formation of volcanoes and earthquakes, they talk about the movement of tectonic plates. These plates are solid pieces of the Earth's crust.

Geologists think of the Earth's crust as having two types of tectonic plates: those that form the land or continents, and those that form the sea or ocean floor.

Tectonic plates are constantly moving around the planet as they float on a layer of molten rock called magma. The heat moving from the centre of the Earth is constantly heating the uppermost rocks of the mantle and melting them.

The lines on this map show Earth's tectonic plates.

The San Andreas Fault in California, USA, is the boundary between two tectonic plates. The movement between the plates can cause earthquakes.

As the tectonic plates are very heavy, they move slowly, only a few centimetres or so a year. When these floating plates collide, there may be up and down movement or side to side movement.

The edges of the plates are called fault lines. Although we cannot feel the movement of most tectonic plates, the movement causes most of the Earth's volcanoes and earthquakes. These volcanoes and earthquakes occur on the fault lines and can have devastating consequences for people.

Chapter 2

Exploding Earth

There are nearly 800 active volcanoes in the world today.
Almost 20 per cent of the world's population lives in the
danger range of an active volcano. When a volcano erupts,
the impact on the environment and people can be
catastrophic.

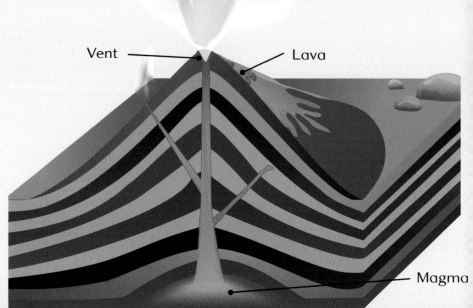

Parts of a volcano

Vent

Lava

Magma

An active volcano in Mexico, which sits on the North American Plate.

Active volcanoes are mostly in areas of the world where tectonic plates join. When plates break or move apart, the hot molten rock called magma can rise from deep within the Earth's interior. When magma flows out of a volcano, it is called lava.

Types of volcanoes

Active These volcanoes are likely to erupt.

Dormant These volcanoes have not erupted for a long time, but still might.

Extinct These volcanoes have not erupted for more than 10,000 years.

Danger zone: Volcanoes

Volcanoes can explode suddenly into the air, covering villages, people, livestock and crops with rocks and poisonous ash. Boiling hot, slow-moving lava can engulf roads, cars, buildings and houses, destroying everything in its path.

Mount Vesuvius in Italy is one of the most dangerous volcanoes in the world because it is so close to Naples, a city of three million people. Mount Vesuvius last erupted in 1944, destroying three villages.

Even more deadly are volcanic explosions of hot ash, gases and lava that flow at great speeds of up to 480 kilometres per hour and can reach temperatures of 1000 degrees Celsius.

ICELAND

Iceland has many active volcanoes. The country straddles two tectonic plates that are pulling apart. Magma rises to the surface, filling in the gaps between the two plates.

A volcanic eruption directly affects people who live nearby. But sometimes people who live a long way from the volcano can be affected by it, too.

Several hundred years ago, the eruption of the Laki volcano made the sky darker over Europe for years. Without light, crops could not grow and it led to widespread famine.

Iceland's Laki volcano today

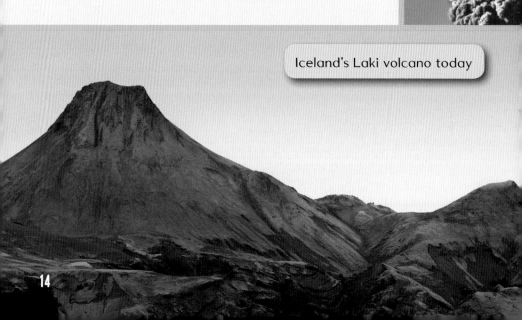

This thick volcanic ash cloud from a volcano in Iceland disrupted air travel in 2010.

In 2010, strong winds carried a huge ash cloud from a volcano in Iceland across mainland Europe. Thousands of flights were cancelled because volcanic ash can damage the engines of aeroplanes and cause them to stop working.

Hot spots

Volcanic activity is not only found at the edges of the tectonic plates. It is also found on the ocean floor and other parts of the Earth's surface, not just at plate boundaries. These places are called hot spots.

A hot spot happens when hot rock rises through the Earth's mantle in a large column. The heat from the large column of hot rock causes rocks beneath the tectonic plate to melt and spread out. This molten magma pushes through the tectonic plate to form volcanoes on the ocean floor or on land.

The large column of hot rock does not shift position over time. As the plate above the hot spot moves, a string of volcanoes is created.

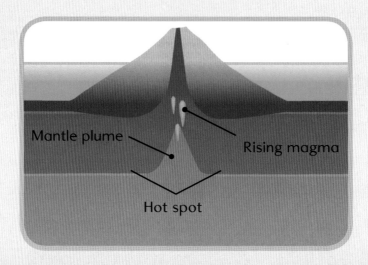

Mantle plume

Rising magma

Hot spot

HAWAII

The Hawaiian islands are located on a hot spot and they are the home of five active volcanoes. These volcanoes have been active for 70 million years. The volcanic activity in this hot spot has produced a chain of volcanoes that runs 6000 kilometres across the Pacific Ocean.

Over the next 10,000 to 100,000 years, another island will appear in the chain. This island has started to form beneath sea level. It is currently about 90 metres below sea level, gradually getting taller with each eruption.

Kilauea on the island of Hawaii is one of the world's most active volcanoes. It has been erupting continuously since 1983. Scientists constantly monitor the lava flows.

YELLOWSTONE NATIONAL PARK

Yellowstone National Park in the United States is a hot spot. Volcanoes first erupted here two million years ago, spewing ash and gas for hundreds of kilometres. The whole area is still considered an active volcano. If it erupts, it will be catastrophic.

Castle Geyser in Yellowstone National Park in the US erupts with steam every 10 to 12 hours.

Bubbles popping on a boiling mud pool

The park's hot springs and boiling mud pools are evidence of the active magma that lies close to the surface, only five kilometres under the ground.

The moving magma has created cracks and vents in the Earth's crust, which allows the groundwater to seep down and heat up. This creates steam vents and over 500 geysers at the park.

Geysers

A geyser is a jet of boiling water and steam that can explode out of the ground.

A geyser forms when water on the Earth's surface flows underground. The cool water eventually reaches water that has been heated to boiling point from the super hot rocks deep below.

An eruption of the Old Faithful Geyser in Yellowstone National Park

The cool water pushes down onto the boiling water, which causes the temperature of the water below the ground to rise even higher, creating steam. The pressure builds until it bursts out of the narrow vent in the ground as a spectacular jet of steam and boiling water. The process of geyser formation can take anywhere from a few hours to many years.

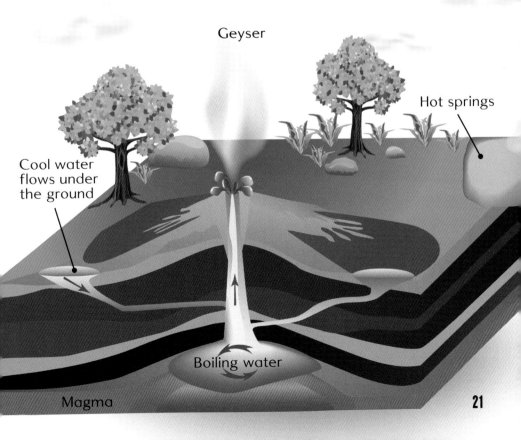

Geyser

Hot springs

Cool water flows under the ground

Boiling water

Magma

Chapter 3
Shaking Earth

An earthquake is a sudden, violent shaking of the ground. It is another reminder of our active planet. The Earth experiences several million earthquakes every year. Many earthquakes are not noticed because they are so small or occur in remote locations, but some can be catastrophic.

A 2008 earthquake in China killed 87, 000 people. It measured 7.9 on the Richter scale. The Richter scale measures the size of earthquakes from 0 to 10.

Earthquakes occur around the joins of tectonic plates when one plate grinds against another. The sliding and grinding are barely noticeable until the build up of pressure between the plates is suddenly released and creates vibrations. These waves of energy shake the Earth's crust, causing an earthquake.

Danger zone: Earthquakes

Earthquakes affect two million people each year. During an earthquake, when the ground is shaking, there are many dangers. Every year about 10,000 people die in earthquakes, with most being killed when buildings collapse on them.

More than 37 million people live in Tokyo, Japan. Its buildings have been designed to withstand earthquakes.

Some countries are more likely to experience earthquakes than others. Japan, which is on the edge of the Pacific Plate, is more likely to experience earthquakes than any other country.

Today, we have the knowledge, technology and shock-absorbing materials to design and construct buildings that can withstand the sideways movement that happens when there is a major earthquake. But, in some places, buildings are poorly constructed. Earthquakes in these places often cause many more deaths because the buildings collapse more easily.

HAITI, 2010

One of the worst recent earthquakes occurred in the country of Haiti in 2010. Although Haiti is on a major fault line, there had not been a major earthquake there in the last 250 years and people were unprepared. Many of the buildings in Haiti are not built to withstand earthquakes and people had little possibility of staying safe when the earthquake struck.

Immediately after the earthquake in Haiti, people emerged to see the destruction.

The earthquake hit near the densely populated capital city of Port-au-Prince. Over 200,000 people were killed, approximately 300,000 people were injured and more than one million people were left homeless because their homes were badly damaged or destroyed.

Today, thousands of survivors of the earthquake are still living in makeshift camps because their homes have not been rebuilt.

A big tent city for the victims of the 2010 earthquake in Port-au-Prince, Haiti.

Tsunamis

Earthquakes also occur deep under the ocean floor.
When this happens, they can generate giant waves called
tsunamis that can devastate coastal communities.

In 2004, a huge undersea earthquake off the coast
of Indonesia displaced 30 trillion litres of water and
triggered a massive tsunami across the Indian Ocean.
Fifteen minutes after the earthquake, giant waves hit
parts of Indonesia. Two hours after the earthquake, the
tsunami reached Sri Lanka, India and Thailand. Seven
hours after the earthquake, it reached the coast of Africa.

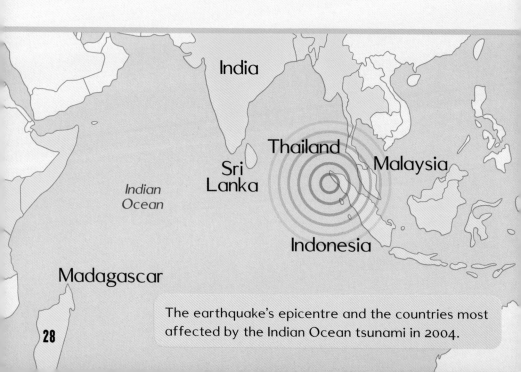

India

Thailand

Sri
Lanka

Malaysia

Indian
Ocean

Indonesia

Madagascar

The earthquake's epicentre and the countries most
affected by the Indian Ocean tsunami in 2004.

The tsunami travelled at speeds of up to 800 kilometres an hour and, when it reached the shore, the waves were 30 metres high in some places. The waves travelled over one kilometre inland. People were swept away in the water, which arrived quickly with little warning. More than 250,000 people were killed and two million people were left homeless. Coastal communities in 13 countries were devastated.

The coast of southern India after the tsunami hit.

Conclusion

The Earth has always been constantly in motion – shifting, sliding and exploding. Its movement causes volcanoes, earthquakes and tsunamis that have devastating consequences, including loss of life and destruction of homes. For thousands of years, people have lived in places that are susceptible to earthquakes and near volcanoes. Over time, many of these communities have become safer. Stricter building codes ensure that new buildings are better able to withstand earthquakes. Safety features are added to old buildings to make them more earthquake resistant, too. They are designed to prevent the total collapse of buildings and to preserve lives.

The San Francisco Bay area in the United States is susceptible to earthquakes.

The Transamerica Pyramid in San Francisco is designed to sway from side to side during an earthquake, while the building remains undamaged.

Advances in technology have helped make communities safer. Scientists can detect when a volcano is about to erupt so people who live nearby can be evacuated.

In Japan, an early warning system for earthquakes slows down trains and sends an alarm to every cell phone in the country. Tsunami warning systems alert people in countries bordering the oceans of approaching tsunamis.

Throughout the world, scientists will continue to work on improving ways to reduce the damage and loss of life from disasters caused by our active Earth.

Glossary

core a solid hot ball of metal at the centre of the Earth

crust the surface of the Earth

epicentre the part of the Earth's surface that is directly above the place an earthquake starts

eruption when lava, steam and ash come out of a volcano

fault lines the edges of tectonic plates

hot spot a place where the Earth's crust is thinner and the magma is close to the surface

lava hot liquid rock that erupts from a volcano

magma hot molten rock below the surface of the Earth

mantle the middle layer of rock and magma between the Earth's crust and core

molten melted by heat

tectonic plates the slabs of rock that make up the Earth's surface

tsunami a very large, high wave, usually caused by an earthquake under the sea, that can cause destruction when it reaches land